Demystifying Death

A Celebration of Life

Preandra Noel

In honor, appreciation, and celebration of

Nobuko Noel

Orlando Omar Noel

Daisaku Ikeda

James O'Neil Spady

Mitsu Hashimoto

Ilene Brown

Henry Noel

John Haydon

Yoshimasa and Sumi Yamamoto

and everyone who I know, have had the pleasure of crossing paths
with, and will get to know.

Thank you.

Table of Contents

To be honest, I don't think that this book needs one because these poems, in and of itself, have no organization other than the fact that they came out of my life when they did. They are part and parcel to a grieving process; an unpredictable and equally messy reality that also influences other ones. By not having a table of contents, I hope to challenge the idea of the unspoken need to make stories "digestable" or into manageable chunks when sometimes they just aren't like that.

Getting to Know the Unknown and Graduating from My Fear of Nothingness

As far as I could fathom, I have always been aware of the inevitability of death. However, with the passage of time, I am realizing that though I might have been aware of its inevitability, my mom's passing on May 11, 2017 at the age of 52 (I was 21) was what truly began to illuminate how unaware I was of death and dying. *What does it mean to die?* — a question that I subconsciously reserved to address for later in life now lingering over me like a storm cloud with its ambiguity; not knowing whether it would rain or if the sun would part the clouds. The weather on the day that I came to know of her passing was a reflection of this limbo; the settling in of an uncertainty of what could come next for a motherless daughter.

Death reawakens this feeling within me every time it comes around. I find myself reacquainting with it as I attempt to understand its actions when it overtly makes its move and also get to know it on its less extroverted days. I don't know if I will ever get used to its company, but at least now I can say that when Death comes to visit I have an appreciation for its appetite, which is not more or less voracious than Life's (or my most hungry self), but equally voracious and non-discriminatory. Death does not take that which Life has given, rather simply accepts Life's gift with the same grace as Life's compassionate gesture--a precious gift-giving between friends often mistaken as a heartless transaction. With this in mind, I write to myself with the hopes that I can commit to remembering the significance of Death's grip, the impact of its unforgettable stories, and its dignity.

+

In the months following my mom's death, I spent my time grieving through my Capstone--the culminating academic, intellectual project of my undergraduate degree. As a junior preparing to go into my senior year, exploring and writing about death was not a topic that I had considered for fulfilling this graduation requirement until my mom passed. In the face of her death and a desperation to find a Capstone topic that could draw my scattered attention towards graduating and moving forward, I mystically dove head first into my grieving process with the hope of finding a sense of closure for something that I knew had left what felt like an unable to be sealed, gaping wound in my heart. With the support of a loving community of people including family and friends alike, both within and outside the walls of the university, and a wonderful Capstone mentor to guide me in this pursuit, I was able to hold space for myself and analyze the larger philosophical point about death and my own relationship to it. For the creative piece of my Capstone project, I decided to proactively grapple with my denial—my inability to understand and accept my mom's passing by writing poems as much as I could during the span of my senior year. My poems are, in hindsight, a documentation of the ebbs and flows of my feelings and the fleeting and spontaneous moments and experiences that could so easily have been forgotten had I not written them down.

As a result of this educational, life-expanding endeavor to find a sense of what I assumed would be closure, I began to welcome a new beginning, immerse into a broader understanding of this integral friend of Life, and find another voice through poetry which has helped me cope through my loss and losses. These poems might not make any sense or resonate with you, but I hope that this book can provide another perspective on grief or simply be another exposure to the plethora of diverse experiences of being human. As a side note, a majority of the photos that I chose to include are of flowers that I encountered on my walks living in the East Coast, which is where I moved to a month after graduating. They bring me joy whenever I see them and embody the beauty of the transience of existence. They also remind me of the words by a 13th century Japanese Buddhist religious reformer named Nichiren Daishonin who says that "winter always turns to spring".

Before

Fear was imaginary.

The world, make-believe.

But now, they're real.

For I have brought it into existence.

By fearing myself, my life

without you.

After

Fear is imaginary.

The world, a metaphor.

And still, they're real.

For I have participated in the experience

By loving myself, my life

still with you.

1. Voracious

It exists
in my veins and in my bones
Eating

The more time passes
I forget
to feel it
Eating

In the depths of my darkest thoughts
it sits there
Eating

In the bloody pool of feelings
it swims there
Eating

Eating It
Eating Them
preparing to eat
Me

I cry because…

I feel its hunger
I hear Their pain
I know it's real

But I mustn't forget
to let go
Because I too eat

and whether I like it or not
it's one of my greatest blessings

10.17.17

2. I Hate Days Like Today

We're all going through shit.
Deep shit.

You know it

You're not the same
You never will be

Different You are
and that will never
change
Does that scare You? I ask myself
To which I respond, I must
change

When can I bask in your glories and feel the warmth of shame?
And to that She says,
change
Melanin into White
Light into Dark
And You will see…
      But I don't want to.

I am motherless.

And You will see that
You're just going to have to
Deal with it.
Because time doesn't heal
change does
And you're trying too hard to stay the same

10.18.17

3. Just Say It

I wish I had the courage to say
I don't
        have a thought
        want to talk
                right now
It's not you
        or me
                It's us

See.
        the reserved tears of the land
        the wildfire's fury
Hear.
        the screams and the silence
Taste.
        the empty words
Feel.
        Sorry
                for just a moment

and laugh

Because it's more than ok
and you won't always be ready

4. Goodnight Wishes

Tonight again
I cannot sleep
Because the thought of seeing You again troubles me

I want to see You
But

I'm afraid to think about what it will feel like when I wake
When sunlight's kiss burns me
but my heart continues to beat
When the bluebird's song tells me that I'm living the nightmare
but I cannot sleep

Moonlight
Thou shall not call
For I will only cry at your beauty

I ask for light in the form of color
Because
Darkness, my old friend
It's getting darker in this little heart of mine knowing

That he
That they
Are not the last

10.19.17

5. Late Night Pizza

If you're stuck on Hope
Turn around and take a left
and you'll find Her
Patiently waiting
        after you arrive
        with two boxes

of words, thoughts and flavors
that She wants you to hold onto
        for just a few more seconds
as She melts in your palm and into your arms

Dissolving
Everything else
        into a delicious cinnamon roll
                Giving Her the zests of life again
For there are no curfews for hot nights like these with nameless
strangers

Caught
Unexpectedly by a delivery,
"Nice earrings"
                and Hope.

10.22.17

6. Today, I accept.

I am awake
And I cannot move.

Paralyzed
Under a layer of bricks and stones

Painless
But my pillow a wet sponge.

I, fall deeper
Bones breaking

Into fragments that can't be put back together

Bleeding on the inside.

I become Nothing
But ashes
That are scattered into the deep blue

Everything seems pointless.
As I lay there
Plagued by Intellect
Calmed by Madness

And I felt
My bed hugging me, the way my mom did.
And I didn't want to leave.
Because I was comfortable.
Withdrawing from reality and taking a break
Knowing that
I could wander through the hidden valleys of personal freedom

Temporarily exit
this schizophrenic world.
That She is no longer in.
Allow my little dream world to be shattered
As I embrace
You
As part of my story.

10.23.17

二十

7. Cancer

I can survive this ordeal

I can surpass this misery

I can serve as your host

But remember,
This is war.

Conquered,
Not I.
Surrender,
Not I.

Timeless is my winning spirit.

10.24.17

8. The One Who Fears Chaos

I don't know who you are
But you're watching me
Surveilling us
like God
Playing a song for us
that's on repeat for 24 hours
with a ukulele
Making us believe that you control the monsters in our heads
when you're creating them with
your gaze

What you see and hear is
Incomplete
Posters that speak through silence
Protests that speak through resistance
Anonymity

Your panopticon is limited
Try and interpret our inner narrative and you'll find that you can't
Because we're whispering down below
Silently
And there is something monitoring your every move too
Leaving us
free to imagine what you are through blurry photos of gossip
for entertainment
Giving us the right to leave before the end of the show
To wreak havoc

10.24.17

二十二

9. Shy Moon

It's all in my head.
Demons and fairies and
Marinara pasta with parmesan cheese

He came forward and told me that
He doesn't remember
dreaming of me last night.

I do
And I'm still there.

Standing, wet after the rain
in the dark
My tears, a fluorescent glow
Bittersweet with memories of a lost forest
that I'm in.
Alone

Throwing up
my hands to that familiar stranger on the other side
Trying to leave
tasteless recollections behind
The open doors of a new territory where stars are a rosy
red and a basket of poisonous apples that
smell of rabbit blood and night time amour

And the sun is preoccupied with the moon.

10.25.17

10. Bella

Youngsters make me giggle.

They say the best things.
They're curious.
And they draw you things.

You ask them to draw you a cat
And they will.

At first,
            they'll draw you something that looks like a seal.
It's nothing unsightly, just different than usual
And as you get ready to ask them a couple of questions about it
            they will erase it.
You wonder why, but you don't question them because you did ask
them for a cat.
Cats aren't missing a pair of ears, a triangular nose
A tail.

Their ability to make monstrous creatures look cute
Reminds me of why I want to be a kid again

Confidence breathes once more when they pick up their marker
This time around they start with a circle that has a happy face
inside, two long toothpick legs
            and two branches for arms
An imperishable snowman already missing some parts
            in this scorching, hot weather

They look at you when they're done
And you can't help but giggle again
Because
Well…

It still can't hear or smell
and doesn't have a tail.

You show them how you draw yours.
They copy and paste some things they like.
And when they remember to draw the tail
you guffaw

Because they draw a penis.

10.25.17

11. It Must Be a Girl Crush

I deeply admire the girl next door
She makes my heart flutter
        Like butterflies in the spring
She is
kind
beautiful
intelligent
        a hot cup of cocoa on a Friday night
Her long black hair reminiscent of the beauty in the dark
        Her smile, fire dancing on a candle

When our eyes meet
        Loneliness dissolves like cotton candy.
        Weakness finds the courage to call itself Strength.
        I see Me
                and two peas in a pod.
                And it makes Me happy
                        To call Her my friend.

She is better than a boy crush
        Because I can love Her forever.
She is better than a boy crush
        Because with Her love is safe and valuable.
She is better than a boy crush
        Because She fills all of our night skies with the brightest
stars.

And I can't thank Her enough.
        for being

My neighbor

My friend
My girl crush.

10.30.17

12. Hungover

This is not my room.

This is not my blanket.
And I'm on the floor.
Missing
       my Minnie Mouse ears
           my ID card
              my phone
                   and parts of my memory

For a moment,
I don't remember
Awake,
I am shooketh.
Because He is there
on His bed
and I am in His room

I remember now
     Walking back together and
         Wanting to expose my secrets to a fisherman
making his first catch
         Alone with Him, seeking advice from Him,
about Him
               Two bowls of ramen
                 Friends.
                    Beat.

Honesty was shy that night.
        But apparently, I wasn't.

Comfy
On the floor
Under a blanket

二十八

That wasn't in my room.

Dada you might not understand it,
  but I understand it now.
I had fun
  And for a moment
    I didn't remember why.

10.30.17

13. Black Cheerleader

I am a person
I am a thing
I am America

I am a cheerleader
I am Black
I am Liberty

I am left in a basket
at a store

    even though the other ones were taken

Ask me how I feel about spirit
And I'll confidently tell you
    I symbolize value creation

I will not be bought.

11.4.17

14. A Different Celebration

Raining inside
I almost forgot
Teardrops
     12:14AM

Fresh
Lying on the bed
One lover
     10:10AM

Call a friend
See the friend
Privileged.
     11:00AM

Cranberry madness
A delivery
Communication shattered on the floor
     1:30PM

Making my way downtown
With laughter.
Spontaneity.
     3:00PMish

Prayers for you.
Cake and candles for you.
Comfort in the break.
     8:00PMish

Unlike any other day
Because it isn't.

Celebrating You

Today

and for many more years to come.

11.8.17

15. Deep in the Forest

Lost
I cry for a sense of direction
And as soon as leaves carry the weight of stones
I befriend the river
       to guide me
             somewhere else
where my heart can just palpitate
as mind and heart slip past one another

That is also when
I ask myself
Why
The moon gives me hope
       when it can't fill this void
Why
I am greeted every morning by the rising sun
       when I just want to embrace the darkness
Why
I can't do this by myself

And because of the emptiness in me
I tremble,
       Like the Earth.

Only to be embraced by the desire for intimacy, Mother.
       Anywhere I could find it
Even if it's just for one second, Lover.

Finding my way back home to Myself
And crestfallen
Because I know I can't
       See you again.

Found
I cry for a sense of belonging
And as soon as I learn to carry the weight of my stones
I befriend the sky
        to cry with me
                freely
where my heart can just beat
as I slumber

11.18.17

16. Dear Mama

just like the sunflower
I will never stop looking up to you
because you are my sun
and that will never change

11.18.17

17. Worthy to Be Loved

All I did was offer You a cup of hot tea
But it's like You knew
that I craved affection

A touch to remind Me that
I was made out of love
and that I must love myself in the same way
that my mother loved me

Yet,
I had been spending days ashamed of the skin I was in
Because I felt abandoned,
                       lost,
                          alone.

                And the way You relieved my tension
          The knots in my heart
with your hands
Protected Me from getting lost in an opaque cloud of timidities.
Freed Me from the pains of my healing wounds.
Saved Me from feeling what is wrong.

For I have no reason
to be ashamed
of wanting to be loved

11.21.17

18. Stand Tall

Let's be honest.
Flowers are attractive
Partly, because They don't complain about the harsh winters
They express Life in a spectrum of colors
Reverence. Joy. Love. Hope. Sympathy.
And They breathe Death
when I bring Them to Her grave.

Joyfully suffering.
They embrace the transience of existence
Shatter the filters of a genuine monochrome pigment
For They are everywhere
Enticing scents calling forth our memories
Be reminiscent of Them.
Give Them more than plenty or not enough
and They will shrivel up and die.
Share your flood of thoughts and feelings
for that which comes next is still hungry
for time. Your time.
And you'll be left to wonder
if love is a sin.
because You are trapped under the soils of reason.

I cut my fingers on their thorns trying to pick Them
out of the terrain that keeps Them grounded.
Because I too
am not ready to be picked

Because I too
am a flower.
My time is also limited.

Therefore,
Pluck Me instead.

as You put Me in your bouquet
Then, tell Me why I'm there.
      just 'cause.
          I like you.
              I cannot explain.
Then, hand Me over to the beholder that caught your eye.

And I will not whine.
For I too have been chosen by You.

11.22.17

19. Feast On

Mom,
I cut my wounds deeper than a knife, yet
I forgot how to hold the knife with which
I cut the skin of the potato that
Carries the wounds of its travels.
You taught me how to hold it, so that
I can peel fear and doubt off of my hot flesh
And taste the juices that ooze out of freshly peeled apples
However,
I neglected to remember how to hold the knife
Correctly.
because I am stubborn.
And then I remembered You.
There will be many more first times
Without You.
      holidays, birthdays, graduations, weddings, babies.

Every time I,
celebrate
buy tres leches cake from the local super market
pray
You *are* there.

When I,
fall in love
say I do.
and,
pick my white dress.
The moment I
become a mom
You *were going to be* there.

How will I,
know what to do

when my knife is so dull that it cannot cut
the past.
To move forward.
How do I,
let go
Knowing, you're *not going to be* here.
cut what's before me
Knowing I can't.
Enjoy the big feast as though nothing has changed.

11.23.17

四十

20. Unchanged

People say, it's the little things that count
And I believe it.
But these days, it's the little things that irk me.
Anything can get me into a mood and
Everything can make me feel lonely and
The worst part of it all is that it is
All Me.
It is not
      Him or
            Her or
                  Them
It is Me.

Powerlessness clings on to grief and hope
For a sense of security
Strength speaks the truth that will never change

She is not coming back.
But
She is also not going to leave.

Immortality is real
For She lives on
in memories and imagination
words and actions
She exists in Me
      and
it mustn't be forgotten.
I am not walking alone on this
Two-way street
I am happily running a marathon
with other people who are
doing the same.

The biggest blessing is that I will win every marathon
Because She will always be waiting for me at the finish line
Saying
  *Today again you did your very best and won. Now let's do it
again.*

Together.
Continuously.
And death will not do us part.

11.25.17

21. 明るく、楽しく、自分らしく (The Original)

心の中がモヤモヤする
何でだろうと思うと
泣きたくなる

深く考えてみると
答えは心のそこにあった
        始まりには終わりがある
良い事、
そして悪い事も全部
始まりと終わりがあり

始まりと終わりがあるからこそ
生きないといけない
簡単な事ではない

今日から明日へ迎えるのには勇気がいる
希望がいる

探し回っても見つからない時は自分を磨け
それが出来ない時には笑え
人生はその繰り返しだと思う

私は負けない。
何があっても負けない。
負けた日には笑って勝利のガッツポーズ。

***my attempt at a poetic word by word English translation on the
following page

a. With Optimism, Fun, and Authenticity (Translated)

There is an unsettling feeling in my heart
When I ask myself why
I want to cry

When I think about it deeply
the answer has always been there within my heart
               with every beginning, there is an ending
The good things
and the bad things, they all
have a beginning and an end

Because there is a beginning and an end
we must live
This is no easy endeavor

To live for today and tomorrow, one needs courage
one needs hope

Polish yourself when you look around and cannot find it
When you can't do that, laugh
I think life is a repetition of that

I will not be defeated.
No matter what happens, I will not be defeated.
The day that I am defeated, I will laugh and strike a victory pose.

11.25.17

四十四

22. 10 Minutes and 30 Seconds

Run
To the edge of the world
and don't stop
until you're flying

Even if you're unsure of what lies ahead
envision the unknown as your territory
and keep going until it's
all yours

Then, drown yourself in the ambiguities of cosmic love

At first,
the air will begin to thin and
your heart will feel heavy but
Fear not
For Thy lungs
     will expand
          to embrace the stars and moons
              And each and every breath
                    will taste of the Milky Way and
                        a few drops of liquid sunshine

And you will find yourself becoming a synchronized swimmer
       dancing in mystic promises of star-crossed lovers
greeted by a world giving You a standing ovation for
       finding a soulmate with whom
          connections span for all of eternity

11.26.17

23. World War III

Stay with me.
Be with me.
And never leave my side.

I don't
      like
         to
            be
               alone
I don't
      want
         to
            be
               alone
                     for any longer

.

Drenched in rain.
Exhausted.
Never-ending.

Soldiers are losing their battles
in search of Freedom.
only to be informed that
      no one *else* is coming
         and everyone else is dying.

As the sky becomes blue
               blue
               blue
      shadows become gray
                 gray
                   gray

One lone warrior is left
digging
burying
living.
in constant search
for Her.

11.27.17

24. Home Is Your Heart

My name is my home.
My name is my heart.

And each time it's spoken.
knock knock knock

I remember.

11.28.17

25. Dispelling Darkness

Pack fear into your smallest purse and take a one-way street with winding roads.
Spontaneity will take you up a mountain where you'll find a garden of stars and darkness will be forgotten.

11.29.17

26. Mangetsu

Cry
until your present defeat is recognized by your future victory,
　　　your hardships become your nourishment.

For there is no place in this universe where your tears will not
water the seeds You have planted.

the strength exists.
You exist.
and so do others.

Imperfectly round, but shining
in times of darkness.
Blossoming with the moonlight.
Embracing the darkness
　　　in the presence of the sun.

Eagerly waiting for the nightfall,
　　　　　when I truly begin to sprout.
　　　　　Becoming fuller and fuller.

12.3.17

五十

27. Absolute Happiness

Night and day
She prayed that I come.

When I did,
She prayed that I
be surrounded by
  the brightest stars
    the most expansive oceans
      and a rainbow of flowers

In death,
She continues to pray for miracles
and the seeds she sowed are endlessly blossoming

  Today.
    Tomorrow.
      Forever more.

12.5.17

28. Tis the Season

Now it is different
    because timeless is every second
Forever flows
    through memories that bring tears
Flowers with dead petals are framed
    And there are no empty vases

Now it is different
    because yesterday is unchanged
Tomorrow waits
    dressed in dreams and belief
Clouded skies are shining ever so brightly
    And there are no faded shadows

Now it is different
    because stories have no endings
Time breathes
    in healing wounds
Nebulas are found on earth
    and there are no broken hearts

12.9.17

29. Tranquil

Breathe in
oceans, mountains, forests, and evergreens
Free yourself
from fated disturbances

Fear no storm
       because it too shall pass
Then, lock eyes with all of your inner demons
Sign your soul to all your terrors, with nerves of steel

And,
Breathe out
deserts, plains, grasslands, and Japanese maple trees
Forgive yourself
for safeguarding letters deep inside your heart

Then,
Open them all and deliver them to chance
because *thou shall not limit thyself within the boundaries of fate*

12.13.17

30. Heart to Heart

Dear Tree with the red leaves,
> *Hello.*

Did you know that someone looks up to you for nightly encouragement?
> Because if you don't, *I want you to know that I do.*

The way you look under that lamppost,
> standing tall
> scarlet red
> under the night sky
> endlessly glowing
> a fire of some sorts
> within me.
> gently warming my
> insides
> rather than consuming me
> with nameless emotions.
> You somehow manage to
> nurture me
> with a kind of love that I
> really miss

I want you to know that I look up to you in the daytime too.

> As the sun rises,
> I gaze into your luminosity
> and notice that your flames
> go beyond your roots.
> turning into a kind of
> pumpkin orange
> that emanates
> gratitude
> happiness

五十四

and home
sweet
home.

I can see you blushing next to those trees with the green leaves.
Don't *worry about them.*
because you're special.

Sincerely,
A girl with many confessions

12.15.17

31. This Is It

She died.
I just wanted to tell someone.
I don't like the way I'm feeling.
I want her back.
I feel alone.
I'm not ready.
I know I'm not.
I wish I was dreaming.
I am hurting.
I haven't slept.
Because she still lives.
Because I am still here.

12.21.17

32. Two Worlds Collide

In between two worlds.
     I ask myself if I have a place in any of them

Wondering if
     staying in one place for too long
          will make me crazy.
     forgetting one completely
          will make me feel lost.
But then,
     I realized that I am in both worlds.

One plus one equals two,
As much as one times one equals one.

It's all the same.
So, I decided to be courageous.
     to swim in the deepest oceans of the first and to run through
all the lands of the second.

Never forgetting that I am both worlds.

I give myself
permission to be
myself

Preandra

12.22.17

33. Don't Worry About It

What I am not.
You are.
What you are not.
I am.
What we are not.
They are.
What they are not.
We are.

I am
    You are
        We are
            They are
                Not *what you think.*

12.27.17

34. Growing up.

Snakes are crawling into beds and thieves are lurking around town
Innocent little girls and boys are indifferently opening doors and
windows
Letting them all in as though
nothing has changed

And it really hasn't
Stray cats and dogs are still roaming the streets
Mom is at home with true love in the palm of her hands, in the
sound of her voice
ready to serve you the biggest bowl of laughter and smiles

Everything is the same.

Birth. Aging. Sickness. Death

The only thing that changes is you.

12.28.17

35. UFO

They're real.
Like beating hearts and feelings
Unseen from eyes clouded by misconceptions, lies, and deceit
Often times forgotten under the layers of everything else

They're sporadically flying through dark skies like jellyfishes
Scaring all those who fear and reminding the unafraid that there is
plenty unknown.

I remember,
Bearing witness to a star that twinkled in the daylight.
Because when I saw one for the first time
My heart skipped a beat.

12.28.17

36. Five Reasons and Counting

Reasons for not liking butterflies.
One: They're always floating into people's business without
forewarning
Two: Their wings are like an extra pair of eyes that see far beyond
our entire being
Three: Transformation remains unchanged in their cores, leaving
people questioning whether a full transformation is entirely
possible
Four: Insecurities seem non-existent in their beautiful, vibrant
colors
Five: They manage to warp their bodies and enter our stomachs and
then **they tickle us on the insides unexpectedly**

they embody the fragility of beauty, they personify the
transience of life, they flutter at the pace of beating hearts

perhaps, it's because they resemble us so much.
to be honest: I don't dislike butterflies. I just don't like myself sometimes.

Thus, be grateful for butterfly encounters in dreams and
wakefulness because they're nothing but blessings in disguise.

Just a thought.

12.30.17

37. Everything Fantastic

Don't forget to enjoy a playful conversation with fantasy and to mingle with daydream until night. Confidence will come knocking on your door for a striptease and you will *find yourself* immersed in dreams until day and breathing in all the aromas of the moments that make you feel great. And at the end of it all, you will remember that you are complete, authentic, and everything fantastic.

12.30.17

38. A Reminder to Myself

Mom,

Sometimes,
Something tremendously minute
reintroduces me to solitude and gloom.
Rain leaves me bruised as though stones are being thrown at me.
Sunlight burns every piece of my flesh and bones, making its way
to my soul.
Silence screams louder than words
and I drown myself in my own tears.

Most of the time,
Something remarkably great
dissolves all hate into pure gold
creates a barrier of diamonds to protect me from negativity
reminds me of you and the unconditional love you shared with me.

All of the time,
I imagine fulfilling our dreams and goals together.
I think about how your embrace always managed to rid my world
of evils.
I reminisce on the good old days to tap into those moments when
you were there, to tap into my inner child.

This time,
everything minute and great will be ever more appreciated because
I remember you.
    You who have given me strength, love, and courage.
        You who gives me hope.

hugs and kisses,
your daughter

12.31.17

39. Plum Blossom

Why are we here?
Because there is hope.
Why is there hope?
Because we are here.

We decide to keep it alive.
We decide whether to nourish it or let it die.

The seeds were planted in the garden of our mothers' wombs
and we must
never
stop
g
r
o
w
i
n
g

I
will
never
stop
g
r
o
w
i
n
g
until
I have blossomed.

1.3.18

六十四

40. good night conversations

She used to have a sparkle in her eye that made you feel complete
when you looked at her.
It came in a care package with a smile that said anything and
everything imagined can be attained, is possible
she smiled, even if it was temporary

Today, it wasn't there.
At least, not in the same way that it was before.
it seemed lost, in a black hole that kept getting bigger and deeper
maybe even buried, under a mask of false hope that was hiding her
pain, sealed in an envelope labeled DO NOT OPEN.

Miss, where did it go? I asked her.

And then I was reminded that it had never left.
The galaxy was there, right in front of my eyes the entire time.
Not realizing that I didn't see it because
she was sharing it with me,
so that I wouldn't have to face the darkness alone.

1.4.18

41. Greener on the Other Side

Don't forget to tell the ones you love each and every day that you love them. *I love you.* Say it loud and proud because anything and everything will try to take them away, but you are not a force to be reckoned with. *I love you.* You pierce through stones with bows and arrows and start fires with your bare hands. Love incarnate. Befriend your fears with your power. Say *I love you.* Breathe *I love you.* Be *I love you.* Everything is going to be okay.

1.6.18

42. Kasumi

Don't you love when things all connect?
You can feel the thread being sewn from one limb to another,
ecstasy flowing deep within your veins.
The fabrics of your life beginning to interweave with the life of
another,
quilting love for countless generations.
And with every moment known and unknown in our small little
world,
it's expanding us into the universe.

1.6.18

43. Self-Love

Once in a while, believe in yourself so much that you temporarily forget about the world around you. Believe in your world. It's ok to give yourself the time, love, and space to remember that you are not just a part of the world. You are the world. Then, continue to take care of yourself with faith that you can share the exact same love and appreciation with Mother Nature. From time to time, being selfish is the best way to be selfless.

1.8.18

44. Sharing is Caring

There is only one truth.
No one knows you better than yourself.
That's why, even in a world full of people, we feel alone.
C'est la raison pour laquelle unity is crucial and vulnerability is our
strength.

Don't be afraid to share your story
because it's your chance to welcome others into your home, your
citadel
and to share a cup of tea and pastries over all the experiences that
reminds us of why
we're not alone.

1.8.18

45. It's complicated.

Missing you is not easy. I find myself constantly searching for something, someone to fill up these empty spaces that I cannot see within me. The ones you always patched up before I ever even had a chance to notice that they were there. When you were here, there was no room for empty spaces. Never. They were nonexistent. There was no such thing as empty because I always felt whole. Every night, I ask the universe to bless me with a miracle that will make all the pain of emptiness seep out of my pores and into the dry lands hoping to bring them back to life with the same intensity that just might bring you back into my life. I ask it to let me wake up as though all of this never happened, only to be reminded that it all did. I am gifted a reminder of it, of that, every single day. Crying has become second nature because in every teardrop there is a fond memory of you. And all those fond memories trickle into my stream of consciousness reminding me that I am alive, living, breathing, being. They even make me cry over a chick flick that reminds me of all the complexities of love. All of that which made me. Made us. *Missing you is not easy because it's not supposed to be.* I just wish I could talk to you about it. And that just makes me miss you more.

1.9.18

46. Something to Look Forward to

I am an open book.
Whereas you, my dear, are a complicated novel that I want to read
from beginning to end until the sun comes up. I want to hold you in
the palm of my hands and carefully turn your pages without
creating a crease in the backbone of your story. I want to
understand you inside and out through every curve in your body
and feel the words flow off of your skin and onto mine. I want to
read you over and over again and have my breath taken away each
time. I want to learn more about you and the passages that keep
your book bounded, so that I can be a part of your story too.

1.11.18

47. I Am

Do not eroticize me.
If I am nothing more than an object of admiration to you,
then you don't know jack-shit about me.
I am a creation of love, not lust.

1.16.18

48. The H-Narcissism

You're going to love me this year.
I broke through walls with my bare hands and
ran through rose bushes seemingly untouched.
Nothing stopped me and will not stop me
Because today self-love is my mother language.

1.19.18

49. Seashells

In this moment,
I am a wave.
I routinely come to visit the shore because
I miss you.
This sentiment comes and goes, never stopping, leaving behind
lovely trinkets
a trail of memories that whisper the sounds of my deepest emotions
to anyone
who is willing to listen.
Sounds that connect me, connect us
to the rarely seen, the untouched, but the remembered,
to the home that will never change.

And I'm crying
because all I can do is collect and admire what was or leave them,
give them a chance to potentially be something for someone else

What does all of this mean? I don't know.

But I know that I'm not alone. I know that these are not tears of
sadness.
Far from it.
They are some of the droplets that make up our oceans. They are
a part of you.
Tears are being shed because I am the wave and I am recollecting
that you are too.

I routinely come to visit the shore because
I am strong.

1.21.18

50. Fundamental Darkness

As I get ready to turn off the night light
She says, "I am afraid of the dark."
The voices in my head ask:
>What does she mean?
>Is she afraid of darkness itself or of what she cannot see?

I move my hand away from the light switch.

She explains, "I am afraid of the dark because it makes me feel
exposed and vulnerable."
I ask her:
>Why?

She immediately says, *"Dark means danger."*
I respond with another question:
>What are you protecting yourself from?

She takes a moment to respond, "The darkness makes me think of
things."

I try to comfort her:
>It happens to me too. I don't always like it. But I think those
thoughts are, in its own way,
>>trying to protect us.

She looks me in the eyes and asks me, "Why do you think that?"

To which I answer:
>Because I've never felt more awake.

She smiles, closes her eyes, and I turn off the lights.

And that is when I concluded that darkness is just an illusion. It's there to remind us that we have nothing to fear because we are the light.

New definition: *Dark means preserving yourself in a world where people assume they see everything when they don't.*

1.21.18

51. I Just Want to Sleep

It's hard getting out of bed sometimes,
      especially in the winter.
My blanket wraps me up like a warm tortilla,
          away from my problems.
My pillow alleviates the weight on my shoulders,
          and comforts the voices in my head.

Everything here is safe, but that is exactly why everything here is dangerous.
Under these covers, there is no faith in myself, in the world around me
      If I stay too long.
There is nothing but doubt,
      if I get too comfortable living under blankets of wishful thinking.

Honey, get out of bed and your coldest winter will prove to be your warmest spring.
Don't be so apprehensive that you forget to live.

1.24.18

52. The Crusade

Mom, what is unity?
Mom, what is right?
Mom, what is truth?

Is it too naïve of me to think that dialogue can make a difference?
Is it too idealistic of me to think that we can openly share point of
views without being judged?
Is it too stuck-up, maybe even ignorant, for me to say that I am
doing my best?

I just want
> to talk with mutual respect and understanding, even if we
> cry, yell, scream, and shout

I just want
> to learn from one another, talk to one another, understand

I just want
> to break the silence

> *but I'm afraid my words are going to be
> misconstrued for something they're not.*

What do I do mom? What do I do when I'm so afraid that I can't
even stand up for myself in the face of injustice? What do I do
when all I see is grey?

I hear you in every prayer, in every thought, and in everything
around me. *And I realized.*

There is so much grey because the answer isn't simple. There is so
much grey because no one answer fits all. There is so much grey
because we are in the middle of black and white, because we are in
the midst of creating a balance. Therefore, I must not be afraid to

follow my heart, to be myself, and to have faith because that's what you taught me Nobuko.

to believe and have hope for a better world. to believe and have faith in humanity.

1.30.18

53. Butterfly Fly Away

Waiting we are
to transform into something beyond our imagination.
we nestle into our cocoons,
believing we will be better tomorrow.
always seeking hope in despair, victory in defeat
Then we break free
knowing that we are the best self that we can be.
And our flight becomes that of adding color to our little blue home.

2.2.18

八十

54. Cello Suites

When you're strong enough, hear it again.
Tell me how deeply it touches you
Be obsessed and say something, so that I can memorialize your
feelings.

It's not about understanding one another
    Because we never will.
It's about being mindful when sensitivity calls us from home
    with heralds, spirits, and monsters

You are strong, so speak your truth.
Tell your tale of the infinite potentiality of the world in you.
    Try to *understand more than we know.*

And explore the cosmos within.
    Believe in yourself.

2.7.18

55. May I live

You should come home sooner than later.
There is no time to think about it.
There is no time for me to express the matters of my heart.
For me to say that I'm afraid, I'm not ready, and I don't want to go

    because I know it's time.

Stabbed with fear, denial, and the likes from left and right
I look up to the stars hoping that they would provide me with
something other than
You should come home sooner than later.

Butterflies were dying in stomachs before they were given a chance
to fly.
Eyes, visionless and seeing beyond what's right before them.
Kokoro, on the verge of ceasing to play its song.

How ironic.
Holding on to everything, in preparation to let go.

On a beautiful day in May, I went to her, spent time with her, and
told her I loved her.
On a beautiful day in May, I held her hand tight and promised her
that I would bring her back home.
On a beautiful day in May, I found out I was too late and regretted
not having stayed.
On a beautiful day in May, her pain ended and so did my own.
On a beautiful day in May, I was crying tears of relief because I
knew she was in a better place, but I was also crying tears of
sadness because I wanted to be there with her.

You should come home sooner than later.

2.13.18

八十二

56. Almost Real

Good morning to everything that exists, to the world of actuality.
My feelings for you today are bittersweet.
Sweet because she was there again.
Bitter because I woke up and remembered that she is not.
'twas strange
'twas real
'twas everything in between

Until tomorrow, again, sweet dreams.

2.17.18

57. Live

If you can't find the vigor to live for yourself, live for the ones you love.

Spread the wings you have been given.

Expand them beyond what is visible.

Prepare to take flight.

And soar.

Continuously reach for the farthest star until you reunite with her in the heavens.

And, when that day comes, say it loud and proud.

I have lived. for you. for me. for us.

I have lived my best life and I have no regrets.

3.8.18

八十四

58. When You Wake Up and You Have a Strong Desire to Go Back

Disconnected to the world around you.
They visit your dreams because you can't let go
of the regrets that are tying you to the past that can't be touched.
This may be the chance to move on
to abandon the old and embrace the new.
It's ok to miss someone, but there comes a time when you just have
to let go.

3.20.18

59. Fear Less

DEATH

    See
        Hear
            Taste
        Feel
    Smell

Scream it
from the top of your lungs.
loud enough to reach the gods in Mt. Olympus and until you can
hear no more.
Breathe it
until squirrels stop in their tracks and the city becomes silent, until
the entire world become numb to it.
Become it
and watch it become you,
    As you *bring death to life*

4.4.18

八十六

60. 435763

Dear Mama,

For the past few months,   my dreams have been keeping me
awake.   Wide awake.   I dream often, but
it's not that.   I'm wide awake in my dream.   Every morning
I wake up unable to distinguish between dream and wake.   I grow
progressively tired as the day progresses   only
to find myself wide awake in my dreams   again.
Am I awake mama?
            Or is this just another one of my craziest dreams mama?
                Are you really not here? Am I really here?
            I don't know.   Tell me mama. What are my dreams
trying to tell me?   Are you trying to tell me something?
            Are you still here?   Mama please. Give me a sign that

            I have not become a madwoman.

                                                                4.4.18

61. Quiet

Better late than never
Sometimes.

Life taken by a silent killer
Louder than my words.

62. My Conclusion

Dear You,

Remember these words:
Truth, Past, Fate, and Dream.

Life is suffering and nostalgia is our legacy.
Death is inevitable and hope is a decision.

And You must choose to live
        through Her.

                Sincerely,
                        It

4.23.18

63. The Great Mother

When I return to you,

It will simply be

another happy beginning.

With you once more,

It will be again

 another reason for living.

And so we live

happily before, between, and ever after.

over and over and over again

until the end of time.

4.24.18

九十

Background

This longer poem that you are about to read in the next few pages has many blank spaces. They are intentional. I omitted some words from my original piece, which was not a poem.

I would like to take this moment to explain to you why I did so for the simple joy of speaking my truth. At first glance, it might look like I was trying to take up more pages in this book, but this formatting was in fact an artistic choice, my poetic voice, the medium through which I decided to share this particular story.

Within the creative piece of my Capstone, in addition to these poems you have just read, I did my best to capture what I was going through in the form of a narrative as well; creating another opportunity for me to process and expand my understanding of the larger meaning of death at this personal level. In my revisiting of this piece as I prepared this book, I felt that sharing it was integral to this project, but that I also wanted to re-imagine and, in effect, re-create it too.

Part of this desire to change this piece came from reflecting on the habit that I have and am working through of overthinking and over-explaining things that often don't need to be.

To my future self, "There can be a little mystery, Pre".

In this process of choosing what I wanted to share and take out, I found power in myself and meaning in emptiness.

Facing death can feel disorienting and, for me, my omission of some words also symbolizes a scattered mind, more specifically, my scattered mind at the time as I was grappling with my new reality, unsure of whether I was ready to take it on.

Are we ever ready though?

Not Ever Ready

From the moment we are born, we are bound to meet death.

we leave the world with

nothing but our decaying corpses providing no answers as to where

we went and what happened

the dead   only ones who

really get to know death and they don't come back to tell us about

it. How is death?   scary?   beautiful?   what we make it out to

be? I didn't and still don't know. Not knowing

cultivated a fear of becoming nothing--devoid of

something.

my

mama was my sanctuary.

If not to her, with whom do I

process such a great loss?

I think about my mama

she is present in every atom of my being, in the world

around me.

九十二

What is this feeling that dwells

in my heart with an uncontrollable intensity?

as much as I tried, I couldn't run away from it.

this feeling made me sigh a lot, cry myself to sleep, and was here to

stay.   lonely and empty

I have come to appreciate and welcome this

feeling as grief. Grief attempts

to bring about healing.

it won't and shouldn't go away. As time passes, my grief

has become one of my very dear friends.

I clearly remember the day that I received the call

She said, "The doctor says you should come soon. There

might not be that much time left".

there are no words to describe what I was feeling, if I was even

feeling anything.

confronted with   words   I was hoping I wouldn't have to hear

so soon. Life plans shattering in every moment   the

bit of light that I so arduously tried to keep aflame dimming within

me and slowly replacing itself with a void that engulfed me as I

fused into nothingness. This

                              the tip of the iceberg.   all I

could do was sit in my dorm room and pray.   for all

the higher powers of the universe within me to come to my aid, to

provide me with answers, and to give me something

          a miracle.

                              gratitude to   Aki,

for having been there to help me make a decision that I couldn't

at that time; finding the leave of absence form that I was too

overwhelmed and scared to find on my own. With not much time

          her simple yet grand gesture of courage and compassion got

me to book the ticket to fly back to Japan and

see my mama for what I anticipated to be the last time. I was so scared   but   also so

supported.

The truth is that I didn't want to say goodbye

my mama, terminally ill on a hospice bed in   her home

country. She looked so different, yet so familiar.

unable to do anything

hopeless, helpless, and lost, but there. Trying my best to treat her as

though nothing had changed, even though everything was

changing.

"This is all just a nightmare" I told myself.

"I am going to wake up soon," I told myself. "We're going to be

okay," I told myself.

Her condition worsened

However, her smile did not fade. "It's not fair" I told myself

I

knew she wasn't going to tell me anything that shattered my hope.

She masked worry and fear with the warmth of a mother's love,

her strength and resilience,

I put her hands in mine and told her, "I'll

come to pick you up very soon" and "I love you". I made a promise

that, at that time, I really thought I could keep.

believing that there was still time. I remember the doctor and

nurses were surprised at how much my mama seemed to be

"recovering" with my arrival.   I was surprised too, but

九十六

deep within my heart I knew   she wasn't getting any

better.

                                                    I had hope.

everything would be back to the way things were; familiar and

reassuring.

Not telling her goodbye was a way for me to prolong our time

together

Today, I understand   my words of parting carried other

sentiments that I didn't want to express to her then   "I'm

not ready, but I don't want to see you suffer".

afraid to say goodbye.   I   didn't

want to give unforeseen powers to these words that I didn't want to

believe in.

We shared experiences, time, suffering, love, and memories together and I wasn't ready to let all of that go with a goodbye.   the time was coming, but I didn't want to accept that my final parting, in this world, with one of my most beloved people was happening sooner than I could have ever imagined.

          May 11, 2017. Life took me by the reins and changed drastically, unexpectedly, and in a blink of an eye.   I became a motherless child   lost my best friend   a few days after I came back to California wasn't until the following June—after finishing my last semester of my junior year in college—that I went back to Japan to fulfill my promise and to face   my life without her. My 21-year-old self   back on the plane to see her again and, this time, she wasn't going to be there. She   in the urn that carried her. The flight over the Pacific Ocean felt longer than ever

guilt, denial, sadness, and a new kind of fear making itself at home

in my heart.   ceasing to exist, dying, as my heart

skipped   I couldn't forgive myself

   guilty because I wasn't there with her in her very last moments

        In denial

                        Hoping that she was going to win this

time just like she did the last

        Sadness loomed over me

when she died a big piece of me died with her too. I was afraid

        I would become nothing.   terrified

            without her. She

knew me inside and out   trusted with my entire being.

She   loved me with a love so pure and

unconditional that nothing could taint it   made every place feel safe and at home   now dead.   my

safe haven   slowly being chipped away.

wouldn't be there for those milestones anymore.

enduring questions of humanity: What does it mean to be born?

Who am I? What does it mean to be human? What is reality? What

is the meaning of life?   grappling with

the meaning of death.

                                                             growing up

in a community where death is not a taboo.   death

as a natural progression and another phase of a continuum with life

our lives are in rhythm

interconnected. Life   an energy

which has no beginning or end

          yet here I was extremely afraid of it.

swayed by what some might consider the Postmodern Condition.

                                                          mad at

doctors and objective science for not being able to "save" her.

               Doubting what I knew

and who I was becoming because my other half was gone. From

our darkest to our brightest moments, we   lived

through it all together. I never wanted to think about the day that

wouldn't be the case;

                                     alone.

               facing my mama's death,

                  breaking the silence within myself about the everydayness

of it

                                    Does this mean that death

was still a taboo for me too?

                           first ever cancer diagnosis, I

vividly recall being so shocked   I quietly left the room to cry

where my mama wouldn't see me, only to be followed by her and

her warm embrace as she told me that everything was going to be okay—something that, to this day, I wish I had the courage to tell

her too.   cancer came back

                                                                  no

room in my heart or mind to tell her then

not ever ready to say goodbye

                                        saying I love you instead

because this wasn't a *sayonara* but a see you soon.

My mama was and will forever and always be my best friend, my role model, my number one cheerleader, and the best mama to welcome me into and raise me in this world. I miss her more than words could ever explain, but am very grateful because she is now free from suffering and resting in peace. She did not live her life in vain and neither will I. My renewed determination is to make sure that I continue to show my appreciation for her by living my life— this beautiful treasure she has given me—fuller than ever before. It is not easy, but I re-determine to do my best every day because the best is the best we could do and every moment is our greatest opportunity.

Part of My Mama's Obituary for her Memorial Service

Nobuko Noel was born in Kunitachi City, Tokyo, Japan on November 8th, 1964 as Nobuko Yamamoto. She was the fifth daughter of eight children to the late Yoshimasa and Sumi Yamamoto who loved unconditionally, encouraged whole-heartedly, and protected unceasingly each and every one of their children until their passing. She met and fell in love with the father, Orlando Omar Noel, of her daughter (born 1996) and embarked on a new journey to the United States in 1992. Amidst all of life's challenges in her new home where she spent almost half of her life, she overcame each obstacle with strong faith, an undefeated, youthful spirit, a big smile and, most importantly, the love and support of her countless number of amazing friends and family.

She started living the American Dream in 29 Palms, then San Bernardino, and, ultimately, made her way to Corona where she cultivated many lifelong friendships with everyone she met. Nobuko was an accountant at a Japanese noodle company for over fifteen years. She worked hard 24/7 to support her daughter in every way possible. Together, they would do many things—one of which included taking trips to Japan, once every year, to visit family.

Anyone who knew Nobuko would describe her as kind, funny, devoted, hardworking, and strong. She will also be remembered for being Michael Jackson's number one fan, a Lakers fan, a food lover, and, above it all, a great, loving mother and best friend to her daughter. In the summer of 2015, she decided to receive treatment in her home country where she spent the remainder of her days joyfully turning poison into medicine alongside her family. She passed away peacefully on May 11, 2017, after her courageous battle with cancer recurrence. Her ever-victorious life force and appreciation for everything in life was the greatest proof to her winning life, all of which was embodied in her name Nobuko: "child who believes" or "child of faith".

Nobuko (信子)
lived a happy, well-loved, and victorious 52 years.

Within My Prayers

I hear her calling me
Beyond the blue sky
Saying it's just the beginning
Can you hear her too?

8.27.18

Made in United States
North Haven, CT
07 February 2022

15846059R00060